REG· SSMI
ROS O·P

CW01496420

REGINA COELI

CROWN OF THORNS
THE COMPLETE GUIDE
TO THE ROSARY

LISA DE QUAY & DUDLEY PLUNKETT

ILLUSTRATED BY PHILIP HAGREEN & JOHN PAUL DE QUAY

Crown of Thorns is a voluntarily run charity dedicated to the promotion of the Holy Rosary as a means to world peace. The charity encourages simple family prayer, devotion to the Guardian Angels and Reconciliation.

Keeping in mind the great need for peace between peoples, starting with peace of heart for each individual, we ask you to keep the work of the charity in your prayers.

Registered Charity no:1042751

Published by:
Crown of Thorns: The Rosary Charity
P.O. Box 49, Lingfield, Surrey RH7 6YQ, U.K.

Imprimatur: + Kieran Conry
Bishop of Arundel and Brighton 7th February 2012
First Edition 2012

ISBN number: 09549182-2-3

The Complete Guide to the Rosary

**Encompassing:
The 'Crown of Thorns Scriptural Rosary'**

Prayer for priests, our families, and for World Peace.

Written and Compiled by
Lisa de Quay and Dudley Plunkett

Illustrated with woodcuts by Philip Hagreen and
pen and ink drawings by John Paul de Quay

Texts on 'Making a Rosary' and 'The History of the Rosary' adapted
from documents by the late Fr. John Hagreen

Thank You!

To my family for their unfailing support and most constructive criticism during the compilation and writing of this book, and especially to my son John Paul for his illustrations. To Bernadette Laird for calligraphy and also for her friendship and support. My brother Richard for locating prints and Fr. Chris Bergin for encouragement and prayers. Also, Bernard Healey for technical advice and patience.

Above all, I would like to thank Dudley Plunkett and all those whose lives have inspired the need for this work to be produced.

In memory of Granny and Grandfather Hagreen, uncle John, little Mary, and my mother Joan.

Lisa

Dedication:

This book is dedicated to you the reader, that you may find peace.

Contents

THE
CROWN OF THORNS
ROSARY

THE 'CROWN OF THORNS ROSARY'
AN INTRODUCTION

The 'Crown of Thorns Rosary' is an invitation. It is an invitation to dialogue, reconciliation and peace.

The road to peace lies deep within each one of us. Once discovered, it is for each of us to take the first step along it; to build the foundations of a bridge over which others will safely walk. It is not for us to look to others for the answer to world peace, for the answer lies deep within each one of us.

Through many years of aid work two things have stood out clearly in my mind. The first is that wars can be averted through prayer. The second is that prayer itself is a two way conversation. We ourselves must be willing to change to allow God to work.

The 'Crown of Thorns Rosary' was developed to support priests in their work, to bring strength and comfort to families, to give hope to prisoners and for the intention of world peace. Yet the texts can be easily adapted, with the choice of preliminary and final prayers, for any intention.

Enjoy your Rosary, share the leadership and benefit from each other's friendship and company.

Miracles still happen – and they start with you!

Lisa de Quay

THE ROSARY AND WHY WE PRAY IT

The Rosary is the story of the New Testament. Through the beads we follow the life of Mary and Jesus. We follow Mary from the day the Archangel Gabriel came to ask her to become the Mother of Christ, to the day she was crowned Queen of Heaven.

We follow Jesus from the moment the Holy Spirit came down on Mary, through his childhood, his public life, his cruel death on the cross, the joy of Easter when he rose from the dead, to the day he ascended to heaven in glory.

The twenty Mysteries of the Rosary show us God's plan for our salvation. Apart from the Mass itself, there is no greater prayer of praise, reparation, adoration, thanksgiving and petition than the Rosary. This is because it is through recalling the wonders and mercies of God that we are brought into union with him.

It is for this special reason that Our Lady has repeatedly asked us to pray the Rosary, assuring us that we will find the answer to our prayers if we remain faithful to it.

The Rosary is such a tremendously powerful weapon against Satan, that armed with the Rosary in our hearts, and the beads in our hands, we can even stop wars. If we but knew how powerful this prayer is – we would never want to put the beads down.

Our Father

three Hail Marys

Glory be

Our Father

The Apostles' Creed

Ten Hail Marys

Glory be

Fatima Prayer

Our Father

PRAYING THE ROSARY

The Rosary is made up of 'decades'. A decade is one 'Our Father' followed by ten 'Hail Marys' and a 'Glory be'. Whilst it is usual to say five decades at a time, it is better to say one decade well, rather than five decades badly.

Begin with the sign of the cross. Pray the 'Apostles Creed' holding the crucifix and continue on the straight piece of the Rosary with one Our Father, three Hail Marys and a Glory Be, as shown in the picture. Then, to start the first decade, pray one Our Father. Moving on to the circular piece of the Rosary, continue with ten Hail Marys and finish the first decade with one Glory Be and the 'Fatima Prayer'. By praying five decades of the Rosary, you will complete one full circuit of the beads. To finish, after completing your chosen number of decades, pray the 'Hail Holy Queen'. The prayer to 'St. Michael Archangel' and the 'Memorare' are very powerful extra prayers.

As you say each decade, reflect on a story in the life of Mary and Jesus. There are 20 stories to think about. Each story is called a 'Mystery'.

Remember, Mary waits for your prayers. If you speak to her she always listens. She is our mother. When you pray the rosary, begin by telling Mary what you would like her to use your prayers for – and then think about the stories that are hidden in the beads.

THE PRAYERS OF THE HOLY ROSARY

The Sign of the Cross

In the name of the Father,
and of the Son,
and of the Holy Spirit.
Amen.

The Apostles' Creed

I believe in God the Father almighty, Creator of heaven and earth,
And in Jesus Christ, his only Son, our Lord,
Who was conceived by the Holy Spirit, born of the Virgin Mary,
suffered under Pontius Pilate, was crucified, died and was buried;
he descended into hell;
on the third day he rose again from the dead; he ascended into heaven
and is seated at the right hand of God the Father almighty;
from there he will come to judge the living and the dead.
I believe in the Holy Spirit, the holy catholic Church,
the communion of saints, the forgiveness of sins,
the resurrection of the body, and life everlasting.

Amen.

The gates of heaven, closed to souls since the original sin of Adam and Eve, were to be reopened when Jesus conquered death through the Resurrection on Easter morning. Jesus's descent into hell therefore was a triumphant entry into the depths of the underworld. In the 'land of the dead' Jesus now searched for all those souls who had been waiting for this moment to be able to enter Paradise.

The Our Father

Our Father, who art in heaven;
hallowed be Thy name;
Thy kingdom come;
Thy will be done on earth
    as it is in heaven.
Give us this day our daily bread;
and forgive us our trespasses
as we forgive those who trespass
    against us,
and lead us not into temptation;
but deliver us from evil.
Amen.

The Hail Mary

Hail Mary, full of grace,
    the Lord is with thee;
blessed art thou among women,
and blessed is the fruit
    of thy womb, Jesus.
Holy Mary, Mother of God,
pray for us sinners, now and
at the hour of our death.
Amen.

Glory be to the Father

Glory be to the Father,
and to the Son,
and to the Holy Spirit.
As it was in the beginning,
is now and ever shall be,
world without end.
Amen.

The Fatima Prayer

O my Jesus,
forgive us our sins,
save us from the fires of hell
and lead all souls to heaven
especially those who have
most need of thy mercy.

THE ROSARY GROUP / THE FAMILY GROUP

It may prove beneficial if each decade of the Rosary is led by
a different member of the prayer group. The reader of the relevant
decade can then also lead into the first half of the Our Father, the
Hail Mary and the 'Glory be.'

It is important to remember that it is not the leading of the group
that is important, but rather the including of each person within
that group.

In family groups, regular use of one decade a day, with the scriptural
texts and family thanksgiving and requests, proves highly effective.
To pray after a meal, but before the clearing of the dishes, keeps the
family together until prayer is completed.

For younger children, the time between getting into bed and before
turning off of the lights provides another natural time to pray. A
child will normally stretch this time rather than turn the light off!
Very young children will join in with prayers in their own way. It
is never too young to pray. We will learn a great deal from young
children if we are willing to listen.

How To Pray the 'Crown of Thorns Scriptural Rosary'

In the introductions to the scriptural texts that follow, the theme for each Mystery of the Rosary is given in the imagined words and thoughts of Our Lady. These introductions, followed by the petitions for prayer, can be used with the scriptural texts where you find them helpful.

Order of Prayer

1. Initial dedication prayer: 'A Prayer for Priests.' Page 25

2. Follow with your choice of: 'The Joyful Mysteries' / 'The Mysteries of Light' / 'The Sorrowful Mysteries' or 'The Glorious Mysteries,' using the scriptural texts.

3. After the chosen number of decades, continue with your choice from the 'Concluding and Devotional Prayers.' Pages 115 - 117 and Pages 119 - 129

4. Complete the chosen prayers with private intentions requests and a few moments silence.

5. Final Prayer: The Priestly Prayer of Christ. Page 135

Initial Dedication

Prayer for Priests

Lord Jesus, you have chosen your priests from among us and sent them out to proclaim your word and to act in your name. For so great a gift to your Church, we give you praise and thanksgiving. We ask you to fill them with the fire of your love, that their ministry may reveal your presence in the Church.

Since they are earthen vessels, we pray that your power shine out through their weakness. In their afflictions let them never be crushed; in their doubts never despair; in temptation never be destroyed; in persecution never abandoned. Inspire them through prayer to live each day the mystery of your dying and rising.

In times of weakness send them your Spirit, and help them to praise your heavenly Father and pray for poor sinners. By the same Holy Spirit put your word on their lips and your love in their hearts, to bring good news to the poor and healing to the broken hearted; and may the gift of Mary your mother to your disciple John, be your gift to every priest.

Grant that she who formed you in her human image, may form them in your divine image, by the power of your Spirit, to the glory of God the Father. Amen.

O Mary, conceived without sin
Pray for us who have recourse to you. (3 times)

THE
JOYFUL MYSTERIES

THE FIVE JOYFUL MYSTERIES CAUSE US
TO REFLECT UPON THE COMING OF JESUS AS THE
LONG-AWAITED MESSIAH

THE FIRST JOYFUL MYSTERY

The Annunciation

By announcing his plan to Mary, God the Father sends forth his Word, but in secret. He speaks through his messenger and declares his intention to send the long-awaited Messiah.

Mary:
"I am to be his mother. I am willing to serve God in anything, but this is a marvel beyond my imagination: the Word of God made flesh in my womb."

A Prayer:
Blessed Mother, pray for me to be a willing instrument of God in my life. You said a complete and eternal 'yes' without even thinking of the consequences, while I often want to say 'maybe' or 'not yet'. Help me to be of encouragement to others, assured of your support and intervention.

Our Father…

> The angel Gabriel was sent by God to a town in Galilee called Nazareth, to a virgin engaged to a man whose name was Joseph, of the house of David. The virgin's name was Mary. (Luke 1: 26-27)

Hail Mary…

> And the angel came to her and said, "Greetings, favoured one! The Lord is with you!" (Luke 1: 28)

Hail Mary…

She was deeply disturbed by these words, and asked herself what this greeting could mean, but the angel said to her, "Mary, do not be afraid, you have won God's favour."
(Luke 1: 29-30)

Hail Mary…

"Listen, you are to conceive and bear a son, and you must name him Jesus." (Luke 1: 31)

Hail Mary…

"He will be great, and will be called the Son of the Most High. The Lord God will give him the throne of his ancestor David. He will reign over the house of Jacob forever, and of his kingdom there will be no end." (Luke 1: 33-34)

Hail Mary…

Mary said to the angel, "How can this be, since I am a virgin?"
(Luke 1: 34)

Hail Mary…

"The Holy Spirit will come upon you," the angel answered, "and the power of the Most High will cover you with its shadow. And so the child will be holy and will be called Son of God."
(Luke 1: 35)

Hail Mary…

"And know this too: your kinswoman Elizabeth has, in her old age, herself conceived a son, and she whom people called barren is now in her sixth month, for nothing is impossible to God."
(Luke 1: 36-37)

Hail Mary…

"I am the handmaid of the Lord," said Mary, "let what you have said be done to me." And the angel left her. (Luke 1: 38)

Hail Mary…

'All that came to be had life in him and that life was the light of men, a light that shines in the dark, a light that darkness could not overpower.' (John 1: 4-5)

Hail Mary…

Glory be to the Father...
Fatima prayer… O my Jesus…

THE SECOND JOYFUL MYSTERY

The Visitation

God's plan is dimly perceived by Elizabeth, but is gloriously affirmed by Mary when she gives thanks to God through the joyful prayer of the Magnificat.

Mary:
"I felt impelled to go and see Elizabeth, needing both reassurance and courage. The moment of meeting my cousin became the first encounter between the two unborn infants in our wombs, the precursor and his Lord. How precious that moment was to me. It spoke of promises kept, of the great value of human life, and of our destiny as human beings."

A Prayer:
Blessed Mother, the joy of Elizabeth gave you the strength and assurance that you so earnestly desired. Life had changed for you, and you were greatly concerned that Joseph would find the truth of your situation hard to accept. As the archangel Gabriel guided you to the house of Elizabeth, we ask that he guide us to shelter in our uncertainties today.

Our Father...

> Mary set out at that time and went as quickly as she could to a town in the hill country of Judah. She went into Zechariah's house and greeted Elizabeth. (Luke 1: 39-40)

Hail Mary…

As soon as Elizabeth heard Mary's greeting, the child leapt in her womb and Elizabeth was filled with the Holy Spirit. (Luke 1: 41)

Hail Mary…

She gave a loud cry and said, "Of all women you are the most blessed, and blessed is the fruit of your womb! Why should I be honoured with a visit from the mother of my Lord?" (Luke 1: 42-43)

Hail Mary…

"For the moment your greeting reached my ears, the child in my womb leapt for joy. Yes, blessed is she who believed that the promise made her by the Lord would be fulfilled." (Luke 1: 44-45)

Hail Mary…

Mary said, "My soul proclaims the greatness of the Lord and my spirit exults in God my Saviour, because he has looked upon his lowly handmaid." (Luke 1: 46-48)

Hail Mary…

"Holy is his name. His mercy is for those who fear him from generation to generation." (Luke 1: 49)

Hail Mary…

"He has shown strength with his arm; he has scattered the proud in the thoughts of their hearts." (Luke 1: 51)

Hail Mary…

"He has brought down the powerful from their thrones, and lifted up the lowly." (Luke 1: 52)

Hail Mary…

And Mary remained with Elizabeth about three months and then returned to her home. (Luke 1: 56)

Hail Mary…

An Angel of the Lord appeared to Joseph in a dream and said, "Joseph, son of David, do not be afraid to take Mary as your wife, for the child conceived in her is from the Holy Spirit. She will bear a Son, and you are to name him Jesus, for he will save his people from their sins." (Matthew 1: 20-21)

Hail Mary…

Glory be to the Father…
Fatima Prayer… O my Jesus…

THE THIRD JOYFUL MYSTERY

The Birth of Jesus

Through the devoted motherhood of Mary, the world receives God's Son, the Word made flesh.

Mary:
"I held the newborn Jesus in my arms. As his tiny fingers clung to mine I wondered at the marvel of newborn life. This child had entered the world through me, and I was entrusted as a mother. I am his mother … yet he is also my King …"

A Prayer:
Blessed Mother, care for us, as you cared for the child Jesus. You, who held the Saviour in your arms, will hold us in your mantle too, if only we let you. Let us feel the depth of your Son's love for us.

Our Father…

> She gave birth to a son, her first-born. She wrapped him in swaddling clothes, and laid him in a manger, because there was no room for them at the inn. (Luke 2: 6-7)

Hail Mary…

> In the countryside close by there were shepherds who lived in the fields and took it in turns to watch their flocks during the night. The angel of the Lord appeared to them and the glory of the Lord shone round them. They were terrified. (Luke 2: 8-9)

Hail Mary…

But the angel said, "Do not be afraid. Listen. I bring you news of great joy, a joy to be shared by the whole people. Today in the town of David a saviour has been born to you; he is Christ the Lord." (Luke 2: 10-11)

Hail Mary…

"Here is a sign for you: you will find a baby wrapped in swaddling clothes and lying in a manger." (Luke 2: 12)

Hail Mary…

And suddenly there was with the angel a multitude of the heavenly host, praising God and saying, "Glory to God in the highest heaven, and on earth peace among those whom he favours!" (Luke 2: 13-14)

Hail Mary…

The true light, which enlightens everyone, was coming into the world. (John 1: 9)

Hail Mary…

He was in the world, and the world came into being through him, yet the world did not know him. (John 1: 10)

Hail Mary…

He came to his own domain, and his own people did not accept him. (John 1: 11)

Hail Mary…

But to all who did accept him he gave the power to become children of God, to all who believe in the name of him who was born not out of human stock or urge of the flesh or will of man but of God himself. (John 1: 12-13)

Hail Mary…

The Word was made flesh, he lived among us, and we saw his glory, the glory that is his as the only Son of the Father, full of grace and truth. (John 1: 14)

Hail Mary…

Glory be to the Father…
Fatima Prayer…O my Jesus…

THE FOURTH JOYFUL MYSTERY

The Presentation

Mary and Joseph give their public assent to God's plan of redemption for creation by offering the infant Jesus to his Father in the temple at Jerusalem.

Mary:
"Whatever God's plan for my child was, I understood that its fulfilment required my complete trust and co-operation. In love of God and in respect for the law of the land, Joseph and I offered Jesus back to God in the temple. Simeon's words caused me concern, not for myself, but for my child, whose entry into the world Simeon instantly recognised with boundless joy."

A Prayer:
Blessed Mother, may we be swift to recognise Jesus in others, with the same trust and joy shown by Simeon when greeting your tiny child. Fill us with the same deep concern for others that Simeon showed for you.

Our Father…

> When the time came for their purification according to the Law of Moses, they took the child Jesus up to Jerusalem to present him to the Lord. (Luke 2: 22)

Hail Mary…

> At that time there was a man named Simeon living in Jerusalem. He was a good, God-fearing man and was waiting for Israel to be saved. (Luke 2: 25)

Hail Mary…

The Holy Spirit was with him and had assured him that he would not die before he had seen the Lord's promised Messiah. (Luke 2: 26)

Hail Mary…

Prompted by the Spirit he came to the Temple; and when the parents brought in the child Jesus to do for him what the Law required, Simeon took him into his arms and gave thanks to God. (Luke 2: 27-28)

Hail Mary…

And he said: "Now Lord, you have kept your promise, and you may let your servant go in peace. With my own eyes I have seen your salvation, which you have prepared in the presence of all peoples: A light to reveal your will to the Gentiles and bring glory to your people Israel." (Luke 2: 29-32)

Hail Mary…

The child's father and mother were amazed at the things Simeon said about him. (Luke 2: 33)

Hail Mary…

Then Simeon blessed them and said to the child's mother Mary, "This child is destined for the falling and the rising of many in Israel, and to be a sign that will be opposed." (Luke 2: 34)

Hail Mary…

"The inner thoughts of many will be revealed – and a sword will pierce your own soul too." (Luke 2: 35)

Hail Mary…

When Joseph and Mary had finished doing all that was required by the law of the Lord, they returned to their home town of Nazareth in Galilee. (Luke 2: 39)

Hail Mary…

Meanwhile the child grew to maturity; he was full of wisdom, and God's blessings were upon him. (Luke 2: 40)

Hail Mary…

Glory be to the Father…
Fatima Prayer…O my Jesus…

THE FIFTH JOYFUL MYSTERY

The Finding of the Child Jesus in the Temple

Jesus takes the first public step of his ministry, foreshadowing what is to come much later. His understanding of his Father's will is beyond the comprehension of Mary and Joseph, but they accept it, and then begins the long period of Jesus's voluntary obedience to them in his hidden life.

Mary:
"It was not for me to know God's plans. I had to trust, but it was the greatest of tests for us when we realised that Jesus was missing; a total turmoil of human emotions. Could his passion have already begun, and I was not with him? All those years later, the memory of these three days gave me hope as I stood at the foot of the cross."

A Prayer:
Blessed Mother, may we have your help to stay in the Father's will, in peace, despite any worries or afflictions, now and always.

Our Father…

Now every year his parents went to Jerusalem for the festival of the Passover. And when Jesus was twelve years old, they went up for the feast as usual. (Luke 2: 41-42)

Hail Mary…

When the festival was ended and they started to return, the boy Jesus stayed behind in Jerusalem, but his parents did not know it. (Luke 2: 43)

Hail Mary…

Assuming that he was in the group of travellers, they went a day's journey. Then they started to look for him among their relatives and friends. When they did not find him, they returned to Jerusalem to search for him. (Luke 2: 44-45)

Hail Mary…

After three days they found him in the temple, sitting among the teachers, listening to them and asking them questions. And all who heard him were amazed at his understanding and his answers. (Luke 2: 46-47)

Hail Mary…

They were overcome when they saw him, and his mother said to him, "My child, why have you done this to us? See how worried your father and I have been, looking for you." (Luke 2: 48)

Hail Mary…

He answered them, "Why did you have to look for me? Didn't you know that I had to be in my Father's house?" (Luke 2: 49)

Hail Mary…

But they did not understand what he meant. (Luke 2: 50)

Hail Mary…

"If you make my word your home, you will indeed be my disciples, you will learn the truth and the truth will make you free." (John 8: 31-32)

Hail Mary…

So Jesus went back with them to Nazareth, where he was obedient to them. His mother treasured all these things in her heart.

(Luke 2: 51)

Hail Mary…

And Jesus increased in wisdom, and in years, and in divine and human favour. (Luke 2: 52)

Hail Mary…

Glory be to the Father…
Fatima Prayer…O my Jesus…

I have found my sheep that was lost. Rejoice with me because

THE MYSTERIES OF LIGHT

THE FIVE MYSTERIES OF LIGHT SHOW US JESUS REVEALED AS THE SHEPHERD AND SAVIOUR OF SOULS

THE FIRST MYSTERY OF LIGHT

Christ's Baptism in the Jordan

Jesus is revealed to Israel at his baptism. The voice of the Father declares him his beloved Son, and the Holy Spirit comes down upon him to prepare him for his mission.

Mary:
"I knew his going to the Baptist would signal the beginning of a new phase in the life of Jesus, but I could not know how swiftly and violently things would progress. He was anointed by the Spirit, and John's prophecies began to be fulfilled."

A Prayer:
Blessed Mother, may we have your help to be purified by the grace of our baptism, so as to fulfil our role in God's plan.

Our Father…

A man came, sent by God. His name was John. He came as a witness, as a witness to speak for the light, so that everyone might believe through him. (John 1: 6-7)

Hail Mary…

This was the man the prophet Isaiah spoke of when he said: "A voice cries in the wilderness: 'Prepare a way for the Lord, make his paths straight.'" (Matthew 3: 3)

Hail Mary…

"I baptise with water; but there stands among you – unknown to you – the one who is coming after me; and I am not good enough even to untie his sandals." (John 1: 26-27)

Hail Mary…

Then Jesus appeared: he came from Galilee to the Jordan to be baptised by John. John tried to dissuade him. "It is I who need baptism from you" he said, "and yet you come to me!" (Matthew 3: 13-14)

Hail Mary…

But Jesus answered him, "Let it be so for now. For in this way we shall do all that God requires." At this, John gave in to him. (Matthew 3: 15)

Hail Mary…

As soon as Jesus was baptised he came up from the water, and suddenly the heavens opened and he saw the Spirit of God descending like a dove and coming down on him. (Matthew 3: 16)

Hail Mary…

And a voice came from heaven, "You are my Son, the Beloved; with you I am well pleased." (Luke 3: 21-22)

Hail Mary…

John said, "Look, there is the Lamb of God that takes away the sin of the world." (John 1: 29)

Hail Mary…

"The one who sent me to baptise with water said to me, 'He on whom you see the Spirit descend and remain, is the one who baptises with the Holy Spirit.'" (John 1: 33)

Hail Mary…

"Yes, I have seen and I am the witness that he is the Son of God." (John 1: 34)

Hail Mary…

Glory be to the Father…
Fatima Prayer…O my Jesus…

THE SECOND MYSTERY OF LIGHT

Christ's self-revelation at the Marriage Feast of Cana

Jesus tells Mary that it is not yet time for his public mission, but when she tells the servants 'Do whatever he tells you', he changes the water into wine.

Mary:
"I was led by the Spirit to speak to Jesus and to the servants at the wedding feast. The response was overwhelming, but I knew it was a sign for the unbelievers; always I pray for them. How I wish they could know and love my Son!"

A Prayer:
Blessed Mother, pray for our faith, now and in any trials we must face. May Jesus be better known and loved throughout the world!

Our Father…

> There was a wedding in the town of Cana in Galilee. Jesus's mother was there, and Jesus and his disciples had also been invited. (John 2: 1-2)

Hail Mary…

> When they ran out of wine, since the wine provided for the wedding was all finished, the mother of Jesus said to him, "They have no wine." (John 2: 3)

Hail Mary…

Jesus said, "Woman, why turn to me? My hour has not yet come."
(John 2: 3-4)

Hail Mary…

His mother said to the servants, "Do whatever he tells you."
(John 2: 5)

Hail Mary…

The Jews have rules about ritual washing, and for this purpose six
stone water jars were there, each one large enough to hold about
a hundred litres. Jesus said to the servants, "Fill these jars with
water." They filled them to the brim. (John 2: 6-7)

Hail Mary…

He said to them, "Now draw some out, and take it to the chief
steward." So they took it. The steward tasted the water, and it had
turned into wine. (John 2: 8)

Hail Mary…

Having no idea where it came from – only the servants who had
drawn the water knew – the steward called the bridegroom and
said to him, "Everyone else serves the best wine first, and after the
guests have had plenty to drink, he serves the ordinary wine. But
you have kept the best wine until now!" (John 2: 9-10)

Hail Mary…

Jesus performed this first miracle in Cana in Galilee; there he revealed his glory, and his disciples believed in him. (John 2:11)

Hail Mary…

"The wedding guests cannot mourn as long as the bridegroom is with them. The days will come when the bridegroom is taken away from them, and then they will fast." (Matthew 9: 15)

Hail Mary…

"If you remain in me and my words remain in you, you may ask what you will and you shall get it." (John 15: 7)

Hail Mary…

Glory be to the Father…
Fatima Prayer: O my Jesus…

THE THIRD MYSTERY OF LIGHT

Christ's proclamation of the Kingdom of God with his Call to Conversion

Jesus begins to preach to the people to repent and believe in the Good News. He offers forgiveness, healing and many miraculous signs to prompt their faith.

Mary:
"What a whirlwind of action in response to the Father's will! No one will ever know how much he accomplished, but I was privileged to see so much, such wonderful fruit, both in my lifetime and since – love in action, in mercy, in healing – redemptive love."

A Prayer:
Blessed Mother, support us with your prayer, that we may welcome the Kingdom and work for it in thought, word and deed, until we arrive at its very gates.

Our Father…

Jesus went round the whole of Galilee teaching in their synagogues, proclaiming the Good News of the kingdom and curing all kinds of disease and sickness among the people. (Matthew 4: 23)

Hail Mary…

"The Spirit of the Lord has been given to me, for he has anointed me. He has sent me to bring the good news to the poor, to proclaim liberty to captives and to the blind new sight, to set the down-trodden free, to proclaim the Lord's year of favour." (Luke 4: 18-19)

Hail Mary…

"I say this to you who are listening: Love your enemies, do good to those who hate you, bless those who curse you, pray for those who treat you badly." (Luke 6: 27-28)

Hail Mary…

"Not everyone who says to me, 'Lord, Lord,' will enter the kingdom of heaven, but only the one who does the will of my Father in heaven." (Matthew 7: 21)

Hail Mary…

"I tell you solemnly, unless you change and become like little children you will never enter the kingdom of heaven. Anyone who welcomes a little child like this in my name welcomes me." (Matthew 18: 3&5)

Hail Mary…

"So I say to you: Ask, and it will be given to you; search and you will find; knock, and the door will be opened to you. For the one who asks always receives; the one who searches always finds; the one who knocks will always have the door opened to him." (Luke 11: 9-10)

Hail Mary…

"What is the kingdom of God like? And to what should I compare it? It is like a mustard seed that someone took and sowed in the garden; it grew and became a tree, and the birds of the air made nests in its branches." (Luke 13: 18)

Hail Mary…

"Do not be afraid, little flock, for it is your Father's good pleasure to give you the kingdom." (Luke 12: 32)

Hail Mary…

"I tell you, if anyone openly declares himself for me in the presence of men, the Son of Man will declare himself for him in the presence of God's angels." (Luke 12: 8)

Hail Mary…

"Come, you that are blessed by my Father, inherit the Kingdom prepared for you from the foundation of the world." (Matthew 25: 34)

Hail Mary…

Glory be to the Father…
Fatima Prayer: O my Jesus…

THE FOURTH MYSTERY OF LIGHT

Christ's Transfiguration

Jesus encourages the faith of the key apostles by letting them be witnesses of his glorious Transfiguration. The Father commands the fearful apostles to "listen to him". The Law and the Prophets also confirm his mission in the persons of Moses and Elijah.

Mary:
"This was a very great privilege given to the three apostles, which helped them to overcome their human weaknesses, and to stay faithful following the crucifixion of Jesus. Once again, today, it is for his disciples to capture that moment in faith, as they await the coming of the Kingdom, listening always to his words, as the Father asks."

A Prayer:
Blessed Mother, be our Mediatrix of graces, so that we are caught up in this glory in our prayer, and thus strengthened in our life of faith.

Our Father…

Jesus took with him Peter and John and James, and went up on the mountain to pray. And while he was praying, the appearance of his face changed, and his clothes became dazzling white.
(Luke 9: 28-29)

Hail Mary…

Suddenly they saw two men, Moses and Elijah, talking to him. They appeared in glory and were speaking of his departure, which he was about to accomplish in Jerusalem. (Luke 9: 30-31)

Hail Mary…

Now Peter and his companions were weighed down with sleep; but since they had stayed awake, they saw his glory and the two men who stood with him. (Luke 9: 32)

Hail Mary…

As these were leaving him, Peter said to Jesus, "Master, it is wonderful for us to be here; so let us make three tents, one for you, one for Moses and one for Elijah." He did not know what he was saying. (Luke 9: 33)

Hail Mary…

As he spoke, a cloud came and covered them with shadow; and when they went into the cloud the disciples were afraid. And a voice came from the cloud saying, "This is my Son, the Chosen One. Listen to him." (Luke 9: 34-35)

Hail Mary…

When they heard this, the disciples fell on their faces, overcome with fear. But Jesus came up and touched them. "Stand up," he said, "do not be afraid." And when they looked up, they saw no-one except Jesus himself alone. (Matthew 17: 6-8)

Hail Mary…

As they were coming down the mountain, Jesus ordered them, "Tell no one about the vision, until the Son of Man has been raised from the dead." (Matthew 17: 9)

Hail Mary…

"Blessed are the eyes that see what you see! For I tell you that many prophets and kings desired to see what you see, but did not see it, and to hear what you hear, but did not hear it." (Luke 10: 23-24)

Hail Mary…

"You are the light of the world. A city built on a hill-top cannot be hidden." (Matthew 5: 14)

Hail Mary…

"No one lights a lamp to put it under a tub; they put it on the lamp-stand where it shines for everyone in the house. In the same way your light must shine in the sight of men." (Matthew 5: 15-16)

Hail Mary…

Glory be to the Father…
Fatima Prayer: O my Jesus…

THE FIFTH MYSTERY OF LIGHT

Christ's Institution of the Eucharist

Jesus consecrates the bread and wine as his body and blood, and offers them to the Father as the everlasting sacrifice, as he prepares to confirm this new covenant thanksgiving offering, with his blood on the cross.

Mary:

"The wonder of the Eucharist is beyond all human telling and even understanding, except that the Lord constantly reveals himself to those who love him. The Eucharist was the greatest epiphany because of its immense scale, its utter perfection and simplicity; a sacrament worthy of God, an expression of his love that cannot be conveyed in words."

A Prayer:

Blessed Mother, pray for our forgiveness, for not having the reverence that is due to the Holy Eucharist. May we learn more and more to enter into the mystery of this sacrament and sacrifice.

Our Father...

When evening came Jesus was at table with the twelve disciples.
(Matthew 26: 20)

Hail Mary...

As they were eating, Jesus took some bread, and when he had said the blessing he broke it and gave it to the disciples, "Take it and eat," he said, "this is my body." (Matthew 26: 26)

Hail Mary…

Then he took a cup, and after giving thanks he gave it to them, saying, "Drink from it, all of you; for this is my blood of the covenant, which is poured out for many for the forgiveness of sins." (Matthew 26: 27)

Hail Mary…

"From now on, I tell you, I shall not drink wine until the day I drink the new wine with you in the kingdom of my Father." (Matthew 26: 29)

Hail Mary…

"I am the true vine, and my Father is the vinedresser. Every branch in me that bears no fruit he cuts away, and every branch that does bear fruit he prunes to make it bear even more." (John 15: 1-2)

Hail Mary…

"Make your home in me, as I make mine in you. As a branch cannot bear fruit all by itself, but must remain part of the vine, neither can you unless you remain in me." (John 15: 4)

Hail Mary…

"This is indeed the will of my Father, that all who see the Son and believe in him may have eternal life; and I will raise them up on the last day." (John 6: 40)

Hail Mary…

"I am the bread of life. Whoever comes to me will never be hungry; and whoever believes in me will never be thirsty." (John 6: 35)

Hail Mary…

"For the bread of God is that which comes down from heaven and gives life to the world." (John 6: 33)

Hail Mary…

The Word was the source of life, and this life brought light to mankind. The light shines in the darkness, and the darkness has never put it out. (John 1: 4-5)

Hail Mary…

Glory be to the Father…
Fatima Prayer…O my Jesus…

QVID·VLTRA·DEBVI·FACERE·TIBI
ET·NON·FECI

THE SORROWFUL MYSTERIES

THE FIVE SORROWFUL MYSTERIES FOCUS OUR
ATTENTION ON JESUS'S PASSION AND DEATH

THE FIRST SORROWFUL MYSTERY

The Agony in the Garden

Jesus submits lovingly and humbly to the Father's plan of redemption, suffering for our sakes in the desolation of Gethsemane.

Mary:
"He suffered willingly out of his infinite love for souls. And so I accompanied him, in my thoughts and heart, and in the scenes of his passion. Too many turned away, his followers too, deserting him."

A Prayer:
Blessed Mother, stay close to us in our sufferings and trials, uniting us with your son Jesus. Whilst our spirit may be willing, our flesh is weak. Help us to accept these special times with patience and fortitude, and remind us of the grace we have been given in Jesus.

Our Father…

"Now the hour has come for the Son of Man to be glorified. I tell you, most solemnly, unless a wheat grain falls on the ground and dies, it remains only a single grain; but if it dies, it yields a rich harvest." (John 12: 23-24)

Hail Mary…

Then Jesus came with them to a small estate called Gethsemane; and he said to his disciples, "Stay here while I go over there to pray." (Matthew 26: 36)

Hail Mary…

"Now my soul is troubled. What shall I say: Father, save me from this hour? But it was for this very reason that I have come to this hour. Father, glorify your name!" (John 12: 27-28)

Hail Mary…

Then an angel appeared to him, coming from heaven to give him strength. (Luke 22: 43)

Hail Mary…

In his anguish he prayed even more earnestly, and his sweat fell to the ground like great drops of blood. (Luke 22: 44)

Hail Mary…

"You should be awake, and praying not to be put to the test. The spirit is willing, but the flesh is weak." (Matthew 26: 41)

Hail Mary…

Knowing everything that was going to happen to him, Jesus then came forward and said, "Who are you looking for?" They answered, "Jesus the Nazarene." He said, "I am he." (John 18: 5)

Hail Mary…

Then all the disciples deserted him and ran away. For the scripture says: 'I shall strike the shepherd, and the sheep of the flock will be scattered.'

(Matthew 26: 56, 31)

Hail Mary...

"You heard me say: I am going away and shall return. I have told you this before it happens, so that when it does happen you may believe." (John 14: 28-29)

Hail Mary...

"Father, the hour has come; glorify your Son so that your Son may glorify you; and through the power over all mankind that you have given him, let him give eternal life to all those you have entrusted to him." (John 17: 1-2)

Hail Mary...

Glory be to the Father...
Fatima Prayer: O my Jesus...

THE SECOND SORROWFUL MYSTERY

The Scourging at the Pillar

Jesus begins his journey of humiliation under the physical assault of the cruel lashes merited by our sins.

Mary:
"The lashes had been foretold, but their ferocity could not have been. Why did he receive such hatred?"

A Prayer:
Blessed Mother, through our own disobedience, pride and lack of love, we too were part of that rebellion. Help us to repent and to be able to open our hearts to the great love of Jesus. We need your assistance, little though we deserve it.

Our Father…

They seized him then and led him away, and they took him to the high priest's house. Peter followed at a distance.
(Luke 22:54)

Hail Mary…

At that instant the cock crew, and the Lord turned and looked straight at Peter, and Peter remembered what the Lord had said to him, "Before the cock crows today, you will have disowned me three times." And he went outside and wept bitterly.
(Luke 22: 60-62)

Hail Mary…

When morning came, all the chief priests and the elders of the people met in council to bring about the death of Jesus. They had him bound, and led him away to hand him over to Pilate, the governor. (Matthew 27: 1-2)

Hail Mary…

Pilate said to them, "Who do you want me to release for you: Barabbas, or Jesus who is called the Christ?" For Pilate knew it was out of jealousy that they had handed Jesus over. (Matthew 27: 17-18)

Hail Mary…

The chief priests and the elders, however, had persuaded the crowd to demand the release of Barabbas and the execution of Jesus. (Matthew 27: 20)

Hail Mary…

Then Pilate asked, "Why, what harm has he done?" But they shouted all the louder, "Let him be crucified!" (Matthew 27: 23)

Hail Mary…

So Pilate, anxious to placate the crowd, released Barabbas for them and, having ordered Jesus to be scourged, handed him over to be crucified. (Mark 15: 15)

Hail Mary…

Pilate took some water, washed his hands in front of the crowd and said, "I am innocent of this man's blood. It is your concern." (Matthew 27: 24)

Hail Mary…

You are my witnesses – it is the Lord who speaks – and I, I am your God, I am he from eternity. (Isaiah 43: 12-13)

Hail Mary…

No need to recall the past, no need to think about what was done before. See, I am doing a new deed, even now it comes to light; can you not see it? (Isaiah 43: 18-19)

Hail Mary…

Glory be to the Father…
Fatima Prayer… O my Jesus…

THE THIRD SORROWFUL MYSTERY

The Crowning with Thorns

Jesus undergoes the humiliation and pain of being crowned with thorns that pierce his face and head.

Mary:
"They mocked him, for they feared the truth that he stood for. He had illuminated their consciences and they did not wish to see."

A Prayer:
Blessed Mother, where I fear the change that I need to make in my life, bring me the confidence to take that first step. When I am hostile to the intentions of others, touch me with faith and wisdom and fill me with the gift of peace.

Our Father…

The governor's soldiers took Jesus with them into the Praetorium and collected the whole cohort round him. (Matthew 27. 27)

Hail Mary…

They stripped him and made him wear a scarlet cloak, and having twisted some thorns into a crown they put this on his head. (Matthew 27: 28-29)

Hail Mary…

They put a reed in his right hand and knelt before him and mocked him, saying, "Hail, King of the Jews!" (Matthew 27: 29)

Hail Mary…

And they spat on him, and took the reed and struck him on the head with it. (Matthew 27: 30)

Hail Mary…

And when they had finished making fun of him, they took off the cloak and dressed him in his own clothes and led him away to crucify him. (Matthew: 27: 31)

Hail Mary…

Never a thought for the works of the Lord, never a glance for what his hands have done. (Isaiah 5: 12)

Hail Mary…

I will tell you what I am going to do to my vineyard: I will take away its hedge for it to be grazed on, and knock down its wall for it to be trampled on. I will lay it waste, unpruned, undug; overgrown by the briar and the thorn. (Isaiah 5: 5-6)

Hail Mary…

We had all gone astray like sheep, each taking his own way, and the Lord burdened him with the sins of all of us. (Isaiah 53: 6)

Hail Mary…

On him lies a punishment that brings us peace, and through his wounds we are healed. (Isaiah 53: 5)

Hail Mary…

"I came into the world for this: to bear witness to the truth; and all who are on the side of truth listen to my voice." (John 18: 37)

Hail Mary…

Glory be to the Father…
Fatima Prayer; O my Jesus…

THE FOURTH SORROWFUL MYSTERY

The Carrying of the Cross

Crushed by the cross, Jesus shares the fate of the most abandoned.

Mary:
"What could I do but follow him…I could not leave…Yet I realised also that it was both a grace and a privilege to be allowed to follow so close to him. They did not turn his mother away."

A Prayer:
Blessed Mother, we ask you to stay beside us in life, in the same way that you supported Jesus. Help us always to be willing to encourage others, walking beside the overburdened and easing their load.

Our Father…

As they led him away, they seized a man, Simon of Cyrene, who was coming in from the country, and they laid the cross on him, and made him carry it behind Jesus. (Luke 23: 26)

Hail Mary…

A great many people followed him, and among them were women who were beating their breasts and wailing for him. (Luke 23: 27)

Hail Mary…

But Jesus turned to them and said, "Daughters of Jerusalem, do not weep for me, but weep for yourselves and for your children."
(Luke 23: 28)

Hail Mary…

"For if they do this when the wood is green, what will happen when it is dry?" (Luke 23: 31)

Hail Mary…

"If anyone wants to be a follower of mine, let him renounce himself and take up his cross every day and follow me."
(Luke 9: 23)

Hail Mary…

"Shoulder my yoke and learn from me, for I am gentle and humble in heart, and you will find rest for your souls. Yes, my yoke is easy, and my burden light." (Matthew 11: 29-30)

Hail Mary…

Ours were the sufferings he bore, ours the sorrows he carried.
(Isaiah 53: 4)

Hail Mary…

"I tell you most solemnly, you will be sorrowful, but your sorrow will turn to joy." (John 16: 20)

Hail Mary…

Harshly dealt with, he bore it humbly, like a lamb that is led to the slaughter-house. (Isaiah 53: 7)

Hail Mary…

"I shall see you again, and your hearts will be full of joy, and that joy no one shall take from you." (John 16: 22)

Hail Mary…

Glory be to the Father…
Fatima Prayer: O my Jesus…

THE FIFTH SORROWFUL MYSTERY

The Crucifixion

As Jesus is crucified on the cross, the faith of the apostles is tested, as fear and sadness prevent them, for now, from understanding the loss of Jesus.

Mary:
"He died out of love for mankind. He died, but this was not to be the end. I wept, suffering with him, even though I believed that God could reverse this tragedy."

A Prayer:
Blessed Mother, your trust was in the Father. However dark the horizon must have appeared to you, however deep your pain, you trusted that God had a greater plan.

Our Father…

When they came to the place that is called The Skull, they crucified Jesus there with the criminals, one on his right and one on his left. (Luke 23: 33)

Hail Mary…

Jesus said, "Father, forgive them; for they do not know what they are doing." (Luke 23: 34)

Hail Mary…

One of the criminals who were hanging there kept deriding him. "Are you not the Christ?" he said. "Save yourself and us as well!" (Luke 23: 39)

Hail Mary…

But the other spoke up and rebuked him. "Have you no fear of God at all?" he said. "You got the same sentence as he did, but in our case we deserved it: we are paying for what we did. But this man has done nothing wrong." (Luke 23: 40-42)

Hail Mary…

"Jesus," he said " remember me when you come into your kingdom." "Indeed, I promise you," Jesus replied " today you will be with me in paradise." (Luke 23: 42-43)

Hail Mary…

Meanwhile, standing near the cross of Jesus were his mother, and his mother's sister, Mary the wife of Cleopas, and Mary of Magdala. (John 19: 25)

Hail Mary…

Jesus said to his mother, "Woman, this is your son." Then to the disciple he said, "This is your mother." (John 19: 26-27)

Hail Mary…

Then Jesus cried again with a loud voice and breathed his last. At that moment the curtain of the temple was torn in two, from top to bottom. The earth shook, and the rocks were split. (Matthew 27: 50-51)

Hail Mary…

Now when the centurion, who stood facing him, saw that in this way Jesus breathed his last, he said, "Truly this man was God's Son!" (Mark 15: 39)

Hail Mary…

"If you forgive others their failings, your heavenly Father will forgive you yours, but if you do not forgive others, your Father will not forgive your failings either." (Matthew 6: 14-15)

Hail Mary…

Glory be to the Father…
Fatima Prayer… O my Jesus…

THE GLORIOUS MYSTERIES

THE FIVE GLORIOUS MYSTERIES LEAD US HEAVENWARDS AND TOWARDS ETERNITY

THE FIRST GLORIOUS MYSTERY

The Resurrection

From Jesus's death comes the total victory, life that will never again be subject to death.

Mary:
"How wonderful it was to greet Jesus after he rose! The greatness of God's works! The victory of love over sin, suffering and death! This is what he offers you if you believe in his name, Jesus, only Son of the Almighty Father."

A Prayer:
Blessed Mother, how deep your thoughts must have been for the three days that you awaited the Resurrection in faith! You did not abandon hope. The new life inaugurated by Jesus brings joy to the whole world! Help us to celebrate it, and to anticipate the glorious fruits it offers to fallen humanity.

Our Father…

When the Sabbath was over, Mary of Magdala, Mary the mother of James, and Salome, brought spices with which to go and anoint the body of Jesus. And very early in the morning on the first day of the week they went to the tomb, just as the sun was rising. (Mark 16: 1-2)

Hail Mary…

They had been saying to one another, "Who will roll away the stone for us from the entrance to the tomb?" But when they looked they could see that the stone, which was very large, had already been rolled back. (Mark 16: 3-4)

Hail Mary…

As they entered the tomb, they saw a young man, dressed in a white robe, sitting on the right-hand side; and they were alarmed. But he said to them, "Do not be alarmed; you are looking for Jesus of Nazareth, who was crucified. He has risen, he is not here. Look, there is the place where they laid him. (Mark 16: 5-7)

Hail Mary…

But go, tell his disciples and Peter that he is going ahead of you to Galilee; there you will see him, just as he told you." So the women went out and fled from the tomb, for terror and amazement had seized them. (Mark 16: 7-8)

Hail Mary…

Jesus appeared first to Mary of Magdala. She then went to those who had been his companions, and who were mourning and in tears, and told them. But they did not believe her. (Mark 16: 9-11)

Hail Mary…

Peter went running to the tomb. He bent down and saw the binding cloths but nothing else; he then went back home, amazed at what had happened. (Luke 24: 12)

Hail Mary…

After this, Jesus showed himself under another form to two of them as they were on their way into the country. These went back and told the others, who did not believe them either. (Mark 16: 12-13)

Hail Mary...

Lastly, he showed himself to the Eleven themselves while they were at table. He reproached them for their incredulity and obstinacy, because they had refused to believe those who had seen him after he had risen. (Mark 16: 14-15)

Hail Mary...

Then he spoke to Thomas, "Put your finger here; look, here are my hands. Give me your hand; put it into my side. Doubt no longer but believe." (John 20: 27)

Hail Mary...

"I am the resurrection and the life. If anyone believes in me, even though he dies, he will live, and whoever lives and believes in me will never die." (John 11: 25)

Hail Mary...

Glory be to the Father...
Fatima Prayer; O my Jesus...

THE SECOND GLORIOUS MYSTERY

The Ascension

Jesus is restored to his true kingship at the right hand of his Father, and his disciples, encouraged by Mary, now await God's saving help in prayer and trust.

Mary:
"I had to let him go, accepting that I would live long after his ascension to heaven, to continue to serve the community with the prolongation of his love, to encourage the apostles and to pray for them."

A Prayer:
Blessed Mother; as you guided the first apostles, guide our priests in their work today. May they feel your motherly love surrounding them, as they strive to continue the work of the first apostles, and that of your own son, Jesus.

Our Father…

Then he said to them, "You foolish men! So slow to believe the full message of the prophets! Was it not ordained that the Christ should suffer and so enter into his glory?" (Luke 24: 25-26)

Hail Mary…

"I tell you most solemnly, anything you ask for from the Father he will grant in my name. Until now you have not asked for anything in my name. Ask and you will receive, and so your joy will be complete." (John 16: 23-24)

Hail Mary…

"There are many rooms in my Father's house; if there were not, I should have told you. I am going now to prepare a place for you. I shall return to take you with me; so that where I am you may be too. You know the way to the place where I am going." (John 14: 2-4)

Hail Mary…

"I give you a new commandment: love one another; just as I have loved you, you also must love one another. By this love you have for one another, everyone will know that you are my disciples." (John 13: 34-35)

Hail Mary…

"Do not judge, and you will not be judged; because the judgements you give are the judgements you will get, and the amount you measure out is the amount you will be given." (Matthew 7: 1-3)

Hail Mary…

"Do not store up for yourselves treasures on earth, where moth and rust consume and where thieves break in and steal; but store up for yourselves treasures in heaven. For where your treasure is, there your heart will be also." (Matthew 6: 19-21)

Hail Mary…

"Everyone then who listens to these words of mine and acts on them will be like a sensible man who built his house on rock. Rain came down, floods rose, gales blew and hurled themselves against that house, and it did not fall: it was founded on rock." (Matthew 7: 24-25)

Hail Mary…

Jesus said to Peter "Feed my lambs." A second time he said to him, "Simon son of John, do you love me?" He replied, "Yes, Lord, you know I love you." Jesus said to him, "Look after my sheep." (John 21: 15-16)

Hail Mary...

"Go, therefore, make disciples of all nations; baptise them in the name of the Father and of the Son and of the Holy Spirit, and teach them to observe all the commands I gave you. And know that I am with you always; yes, to the end of time." (Matthew 28: 19-20)

Hail Mary...

Then he took them out as far as the outskirts of Bethany, and lifting up his hands he blessed them. Now as he blessed them, he withdrew from them and was carried up to heaven. They worshipped him and then went back to Jerusalem full of joy. (Luke 24: 50-52)

Hail Mary...

Glory be to the Father...
Fatima Prayer: O my Jesus...

THE THIRD GLORIOUS MYSTERY

The Descent of the Holy Spirit

The whole of humanity begins to be enlightened by the Spirit of Truth that had so far been known only to a few.

Mary:
"Now at last I could see with clarity the vision that God had for his people: reconciliation, peace, truth, love and salvation, all issuing from the life, death and resurrection of Jesus. I stood humbled at the scale and grandeur of God's plan, in response to my Yes to the Spirit of God."

A Prayer:
Blessed Mother, show us your Son in his splendour, in faith now, and later face to face. May we not fear the Spirit, but welcome it in the same undoubting way that you welcomed the promise of the motherhood of Jesus.

Our Father…

When Pentecost day came round, the Apostles had all met in one room when suddenly they heard what sounded like a powerful wind from heaven, the noise of which filled the entire house in which they were sitting. (Acts 2: 1-2)

Hail Mary…

Something appeared to them that seemed like tongues of fire; these separated and came to rest on the head of each of them. They were all filled with the Holy Spirit, and began to speak foreign languages as the Spirit gave them the gift of speech. (Acts 2: 3-4)

Hail Mary…

Now there were devout men living in Jerusalem from every nation under heaven, and at this sound they all assembled, each one bewildered to hear these men speaking his own language. (Acts 2: 5-6)

Hail Mary…

Then Peter, standing with the Eleven, raised his voice and addressed them, "Fellow-Jews and all of you who live in Jerusalem, listen to me and let me tell you what this means." (Acts 2: 14)

Hail Mary…

"This is what the prophet Joel spoke of: 'In the days to come – it is the Lord who speaks – I will pour out my Spirit upon all mankind. Your sons and your daughters shall proclaim my message, your young men will see visions, your old men will dream dreams.' " (Acts 2: 16-17)

Hail Mary…

"God raised this man Jesus to life and all of us are witnesses to that. Now raised to the heights by God's right hand, he has received from the Father the Holy Spirit, who was promised, and what you see and hear is the outpouring of that Spirit." (Acts 2: 32-33)

Hail Mary…

Peter said to them, "Repent, and be baptised every one of you in the name of Jesus Christ so that your sins may be forgiven; and you will receive the gift of the Holy Spirit." (Acts 2: 38-39)

Hail Mary…

"It is not for you to know times and dates that the Father has decided by his own authority, but you will receive power when the Holy Spirit comes to you, and then you will be my witnesses not only in Jerusalem but throughout Judaea and Samaria, and indeed to the ends of the earth." (Acts 1: 6-8)

Hail Mary…

"For the promise is for you, for your children, and for all who are far away, everyone whom the Lord our God calls to himself."
(Acts 2: 39)

Hail Mary…

"Those who love me will keep my word, and my Father will love them, and we will come to them and make our home with them."
(John 14: 23)

Hail Mary…

Glory be to the Father…
Fatima Prayer: O my Jesus…

THE FOURTH GLORIOUS MYSTERY

The Assumption

The first glorification of created humanity is accomplished in the Assumption of Immaculate Mary, body and soul, into heaven.

Mary:
"It was the will of God for me to wait with the apostles and to intercede on earth as the daily witness of the life of Christ and of the Church. This ministry continues, even after I was welcomed into heaven. Rejoice with me, and prepare daily for the time of your own salvation."

A Prayer:
Blessed Mother, we thank you for your earthly life, given in prayer and faithfulness to the Father, and for your dedication to the upbringing of your son, Jesus, our Saviour. We thank you also for taking to heart his desire that you be a mother to us, and for your special care for our priests and clergy. You are a sign of hope for us. Keep us always on the way of salvation.

Our Father…

> Then the sanctuary of God in heaven opened, and the Ark of the Covenant could be seen inside it. (Revelation 11: 19)

Hail Mary…

> "Who is this arising like the dawn, fair as the moon, resplendent as the sun?" (Song 6: 10)

Hail Mary…

Like the rainbow gleaming against brilliant clouds, like blossoms in the days of spring. (Sirach 50: 7-8)

Hail Mary…

Send out fragrance like incense, and put forth blossoms like a lily. Scatter the fragrance, and sing a hymn of praise; bless the Lord for all his works. (Ecclesiasticus 39:14)

Hail Mary…

See, winter is past, the rains are over and gone. The flowers appear on the earth. The season of glad tidings has come.
(The Song of Songs 2: 11-12)

Hail Mary…

Show me your face, let me hear your voice; for your voice is sweet and your face is beautiful. (The Song of Songs 2: 14)

Hail Mary…

With jewels set in gold, and dressed in brocades, the king's daughter is led in to the king. (Psalm 45: 13-14)

Hail Mary…

The virgin Mother of God was taken up into heaven to be the beginning and the pattern of the Church in its perfection and a sign of hope and comfort for your people on their pilgrim way.
(Preface of the Feast of the Assumption)

Hail Mary…

"From this day forward all generations will call me blessed, for the Almighty has done great things for me. Holy is his name."
(Luke 1: 48-9)

Hail Mary…

If the Spirit of him who raised Jesus from the dead is living in you, then he who raised Jesus from the dead will give life to your own mortal bodies through his Spirit living in you. (Romans 8: 11)

Hail Mary…

Glory be to the Father…
Fatima Prayer; O my Jesus…

THE FIFTH GLORIOUS MYSTERY

The Crowning of Our Lady in Heaven

The glorification of fallen humanity is accomplished outside of human time, to complete God's plan of salvation.

Mary:
"I am the Queen of Heaven and the Queen of Peace, the Mother of all who call to me."

A Prayer:
Blessed Mother, you are with us for all time, and you seek us out to become witnesses and intercessors for the great work of salvation entrusted to you by our God. You are our advocate and refuge. Mary, Queen of Heaven, our mother, may we meet with you in our hearts, and together discover the love, the mercy and the presence of Jesus in eternal glory.

Our Father…

Now a great sign appeared in heaven: a woman, adorned with the sun, standing on the moon, and with the twelve stars on her head for a crown. (Revelation 12: 1)

Hail Mary…

The king rose to meet her, and bowed down to her; then he sat on his throne, and had a throne brought for the king's mother, and she sat on his right. (1 Kings 2: 19)

Hail Mary...

She is more beautiful than the sun, and excels every constellation of the stars. Compared to the light she takes first place, for light must yield to night, but over Wisdom evil can never triumph. (Wisdom 7: 29-30)

Hail Mary...

For she is a reflection of eternal light, a spotless mirror of the working of God, and an image of his goodness. (Wisdom 7: 26)

Hail Mary...

In every generation she passes into holy souls and makes them friends of God, and prophets. (Wisdom 7: 27)

Hail Mary...

"My Mother," the King said to her, "make your request, for I will not refuse you." (1 King 2: 20)

Hail Mary...

For whoever finds me finds life and obtains favour from the Lord. (Proverbs 8: 35)

Hail Mary...

God made two great lights: the greater light to govern the day, and the smaller to govern the night, and the stars. God set them in the vault of heaven to shine on the earth, to govern the day and night and to divide light from darkness. (Genesis 1: 16-18)

Hail Mary…

Heaven is my throne and the earth is my footstool; what is the house that you would build for me, and what is my resting place?
(Isaiah 66: 1)

Hail Mary…

Full of grace she was to be a worthy mother of your Son, your sign of favour to the Church at its beginning, and the promise of its perfection as the bride of Christ, radiant in beauty.
(Preface of the Feast of the Immaculate Conception)

Hail Mary…

Glory be to the Father…
Fatima Prayer; O my Jesus…

CONCLUDING PRAYERS

The Hail Holy Queen

Hail, Holy Queen, Mother of Mercy.
Hail, our life, our sweetness and our hope!
To thee do we cry,
poor banished children of Eve;
to thee do we send up our sighs,
mourning and weeping in this vale of tears.
Turn then, O most gracious Advocate,
thine eyes of mercy towards us
and after this our exile show unto us
the blessed fruit of thy womb, Jesus;
O clement, O loving, O sweet Virgin Mary.

V: *Pray for us, O Holy Mother of God.*
R: That we may be made worthy of the promises of Christ.

Let us pray:

O God, whose only-begotten Son, by his life, death and resurrection
has purchased for us the rewards of eternal life; grant we beseech
you, that meditating on these Mysteries of the most Holy Rosary
of the Blessed Virgin Mary, we may both imitate what they contain
and obtain what they promise, through the same Christ our Lord.

Amen.

Prayer to St. Michael Archangel

Holy Michael, Archangel,
defend us in the day of battle;
be our safeguard against the wickedness
and snares of the devil.
May God rebuke him we humbly pray;
and do thou Prince of the Heavenly Hosts,
by the power of God,
thrust down to hell Satan
and all the other evil spirits
who wander through the world for the ruin of souls.

The Memorare

Remember, O most gracious Virgin Mary,
that never was it known,
that anyone who fled to thy protection,
implored thy help or sought thy intercession,
was left unaided.
Inspired by this confidence, I fly to thee,
O Virgin of virgins, my Mother.
To thee I come, before thee I stand, sinful and sorrowful.
O mother of the Word Incarnate, despise not my petition,
but in thy mercy hear and answer me.

DEVOTIONAL PRAYERS

The Magnificat

My soul glorifies the Lord.
my spirit rejoices in God, my Saviour.
For he looks on his servant in her lowliness;
henceforth all ages will call me blessed.

The Almighty works marvels for me.
Holy is his name!
His mercy is from age to age,
on those who fear him,

He puts forth his arm in strength
and scatters the proud-hearted.
He casts the mighty from their thrones
and raises the lowly.
He fills the starving with good things,
sends the rich away empty.

He protects Israel, his servant,
remembering his mercy,
the mercy promised to our fathers,
to Abraham and his sons for ever.

Glory be to the Father…

A Mother's Prayer for Her Children

As thou didst walk the fields of Galilee,
O loving Saviour walk with them for me:
for since the years have passed and they have grown
I cannot follow, they must walk alone.
Be thou my voice when sinful things draw near
pleading with them for all that will endure.
Be thou the hand that would keep theirs in mine
and all things else a mother must resign.
And as Thy Blessed Mother guided Thee
O kind and loving Jesus, guide my boys and girls for me.

A Parent's Prayer

Heavenly Father, make me a better parent.
Teach me to understand my children,
to listen patiently to what they have to say,
and to answer all their questions kindly.
Keep me from interrupting or contradicting them.
Make me courteous to them as I would have them be to me.
Bless me with the discernment to grant them all their
    reasonable requests,
and the courage to deny them harm.
Make me fair and just and kind,
and fit me, O Lord, to be loved and respected and imitated
    by my children.

A Parent's Prayer to St. Joseph

O glorious St. Joseph,
to you God committed the care of His only begotten Son
amid the many dangers of this world.
We come to you
and ask you to take under your special protection
the children God has given us.
Through holy baptism they became children of God
and members of His holy Church.
We consecrate them to you today,
that through this consecration
they may become your foster children.
Guard them, guide their steps in life,
form their hearts after the hearts of Jesus and Mary.

St. Joseph,
who felt the tribulation and worry of a parent
when the child Jesus was lost,
protect our dear children for time and eternity.
May you be their father and counsellor.
Let them, like Jesus,
grow in age as well as in wisdom and grace
before God and men.
Preserve them from the corruption of this world,
and give us the grace one day to be united
with them in heaven forever.

A Prayer for Purity

Hail bright star of ocean,
God's own Mother blest,
Ever sinless Virgin,
Gate of heavenly rest.

Taking that sweet Ave,
Which from Gabriel came,
Peace confirm within us,
Changing Eva's name.

Break the captives' fetters,
Light on blindness pour,
All our ills expelling,
Every bliss implore.

Show thyself a Mother,
May the Word Divine,
Born for us thy Infant,
Hear our prayers through thine.

Virgin all excelling,
Mildest of the mild,
Freed from guilt, preserve us,
Pure and undefiled.

Keep our life all spotless,
Make our way secure,
Till we find in Jesus,
Joy for evermore.

Through the highest heaven,
To the Almighty Three,
Father, Son, and Spirit
one same glory be.

Prayer to our Blessed Mother for the elderly

(for protection of oneself or of another)

Take my (his/her) hand, O Blessed Mother,
Hold it firmly lest I fall,
I am nervous when I'm walking
And to thee I humbly call.

Guide me over every crossing,
Watch me when I'm on the stairs,
Let me know you are beside me,
Listen to my fervent prayers.

Bring me to my destination
Safely every single day,
Help me with each undertaking,
As the hours pass away.

And when evening falls upon us,
And I fear to be alone,
Take my hand, O Blessed Mother,
Once again and lead me home.

Prayer to our Guardian Angels

(for protection)

Guardian Angel, from Heaven so bright,
Watch beside me, to lead me aright.
Fold thy wings round me, O guard me with love,
Softly sing songs to me of Heaven above.
Beautiful Angel, my Guardian so mild,
Tenderly guide me, for I am thy child.

Request to the Holy Spirit

To God be honour and glory for ever.
Fill us with hope and with the
power of the Holy Spirit.
Send your Holy Spirit to turn our words
into prayers and our seeking into finding.
Send your Holy Spirit to turn darkness
into light and our falseness into truth.
Send your Holy Spirit to make us your
witnesses today in word and deed.
Send your Holy Spirit to help us in our
weakness and teach us how to pray.
Send your Holy Spirit to bring order out
of chaos and love out of hatred.

A prayer for Wisdom in Government and Leadership

Holy Spirit, Lord of light,
From the clear celestial height
Thy pure beaming radiance give.
Come, thou Father of the poor,
Come with treasures which endure:
Come through light of all that live.

Thou, of all consolers best,
Thou, the soul's delightful guest.
Dost refreshing peace bestow.
Thou in toil art comfort sweet;
Pleasant coolness in the heat,
Solace in the midst of woe.

Light immortal, light divine,
Visit thou these hearts of thine,
And our inmost being fill.
If thou take thy grace away
Nothing pure in man will stay;
All his good is turned to ill.

Heal our wounds, our strength renew,
On our dryness pour thy dew,
Wash the stains of guilt away.
Bend the stubborn hearts and will;
Melt the frozen, warm the chill;
Guide the steps that go astray.

Thou, on those who evermore
Thee confess and thee adore,
In thy sevenfold gifts descend;
Give them comfort when they die,
Give them joys that never end.

Prayer for the Fruits of the Earth

Pour out thy blessing, we beseech thee, O Lord,
upon thy people and upon all the fruits of the earth,
that being gathered in they may be mercifully distributed,
to the honour and glory of thy holy name.
Through our Lord Jesus Christ.   Amen.

For Trust in God.

And I said to the man who stood at the gate of the year:
"Give me a light that I may tread safely into the unknown."
And he replied: "Go out into the darkness
and put your hand into the hand of God.
That shall be to you better than light
and safer than a known way."

World Peace Prayer

Lead me from death to life,
from falsehood to truth.

Lead me from despair to hope,
from fear to trust.

Lead me from hate to love,
from war to peace.

Let peace fill our hearts,
our world, our universe.

FINAL PRAYER

The Priestly Prayer of Christ

"Holy Father,
keep those you have given me true to your name,
so that they may be one like us.

Protect them from the evil one.

Consecrate them in the truth; your word is truth.
As you sent me into the world,
I have sent them into the world,
and for their sake I consecrate myself,
so that they too may be consecrated in truth.

I pray not only for these,
but for those also, who through their words, will believe in me.
May they all be one.

May they be so completely one,
that the world will realise that it was you who sent me,
and that I have loved them as much as you loved me.

Father, Righteous One,
I have made your name known to them,
and will continue to make it known,
so that the love with which you loved me may be in them,
and so that I may be in them."

(John 17: 11b, 15, 17-21, 23, 25-26)

PLEDGE TO OUR LADY AND TO THE HOLY ROSARY

O Blessed Rosary of Mary,
sweet chain which unites us to God,
bond of love which unites us to the angels,
tower of salvation against the assaults of hell,
safe port in our universal shipwreck,
we will never abandon you.

You will be our comfort in the hour of death:
Yours our final kiss as life ebbs away.
And the last word from our lips will be your name.

O Queen of the Rosary,
O dearest Mother,
O Refuge of Sinners,
O Sovereign Consoler of the Afflicted.
May you be everywhere blessed,
today and always,
on earth and in Heaven.

OUR LADY'S PLEDGE FOR OUR PROTECTION

"Here me and understand well, my son the least, that nothing should frighten or grieve you. Let not your heart be disturbed. Do not fear sickness or anguish. Am I not here who is your Mother? Are you not under my protection? Am I not your health? Are you not happily within my fold? What else do you wish? Do not grieve nor be disturbed by anything."

(From the message of Our Lady to Juan Diego, Guadalupe.)

The Rosary for Our Times.

"There is no problem, no matter how difficult it is, temporal or especially spiritual, in the personal life of each one of us, of our families, of the families of the world or of the religious communities, or even of the life of peoples and nations that cannot be solved by the Rosary. There is no problem, I tell you, no matter how difficult it is, that we cannot resolve by the prayer of the Holy Rosary…" (Sister Lucy of Fatima in 1957)

When Our Lady appears on this earth she repeatedly asks us to change our ways, and to pray the Rosary. As any good mother would always guide her children, she is no exception and God allows her intervention and encouragement, particularly when there is danger to us, her children.

In peacetime we must continue to pray the rosary, not just for ourselves but for others.

"I am the Lady of the Rosary. Continue always to pray the Rosary every day."
(Fatima, Portugal. October 13th 1917)

With a true mother's love for her children, she repeats her call, intervening with great love between God and man throughout the ages.

Our Lady gives us courage. A loving mother, she calls her children back to safety in times of danger. The Holy Rosary is the medium of prayer of her choice through which we can reach her, and through which she presents our requests, and most importantly, our gratitude for all things, to God. For God, like all fathers, is pleased when thanks is given!

THE ROSARY FOR OUR FAMILIES

"As a prayer for peace, the rosary is also a prayer of and for the family. We need to return to the practice of family prayer, and prayer for families. The family that prays together stays together. The family that recites the Rosary together reproduces something of the atmosphere of the household of Nazareth: its members place Jesus at the centre, they share his joys and sorrows, they place their needs and their plans in his hands, they draw from him the hope and the strength to go on."

(Pope John Paul II 2002)

PRAYING THE FAMILY ROSARY

The secret of the Family Rosary is to enjoy, to explore, to imagine.

Following the decades, bead by bead, is alike to reading the Gospels in brail. Once children have learnt the sequence of the mysteries, they can then follow the life of the Holy Family, by praying the rosary, even if they can't read. Listen to each other, share, be small. Thank God for all things, both the good and the difficult! Enjoy the light of candles and the silence of the phone being unplugged… Adapt and support in all things as children grow.

(See also page 19: The Rosary Group / The Family Group)

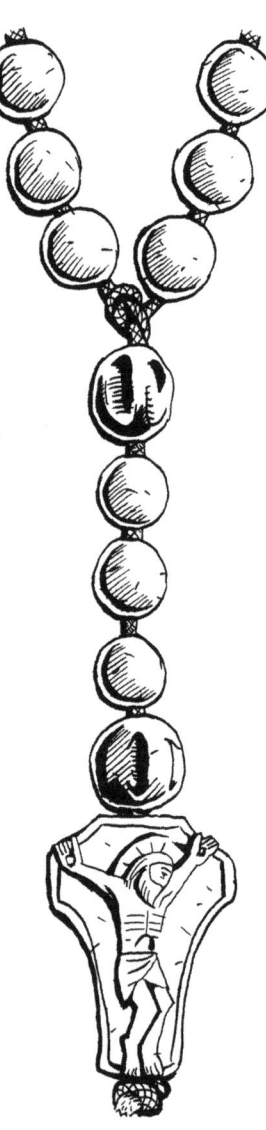

THOUGHTS ON MAKING A ROSARY

Why buy one when you can do a better job yourself?

A rosary designed for carrying loose will have a cross which does not tangle with the beads, damage pockets or catch in everything it touches. The chaplet will be one which does not have to be untangled before use.

Spherical beads are the most comfortable to finger and, if strung and not wired, make for the most compact rosary in relation to their size. However, a wired rosary, once broken, cannot be satisfactorily mended, whereas anyone who has access to cord or string and who can tie a bowline knot, can string a rosary.

If the beads used for the 'Paters' or 'Our Fathers', are larger or of different shape than those used for the 'Aves' or 'Hail Marys', then no other separation between the beads of the decades is required. Simply thread the beads, then, with the addition of a dab of strong glue on the knot before tightening and by using rot proof or waxed cord, the rosary will last a lifetime, provided the hole in the beads is smooth.

So why buy one when you can do a better job yourself? Why not encourage the art of rosary making? At Crown of Thorns we have received many beautiful homemade rosaries, handmade in various countries of the world, made of materials found abundantly in their country of origin. Tiny round shells, dried pulses and beans, or just a simple string with knots.

Shells.

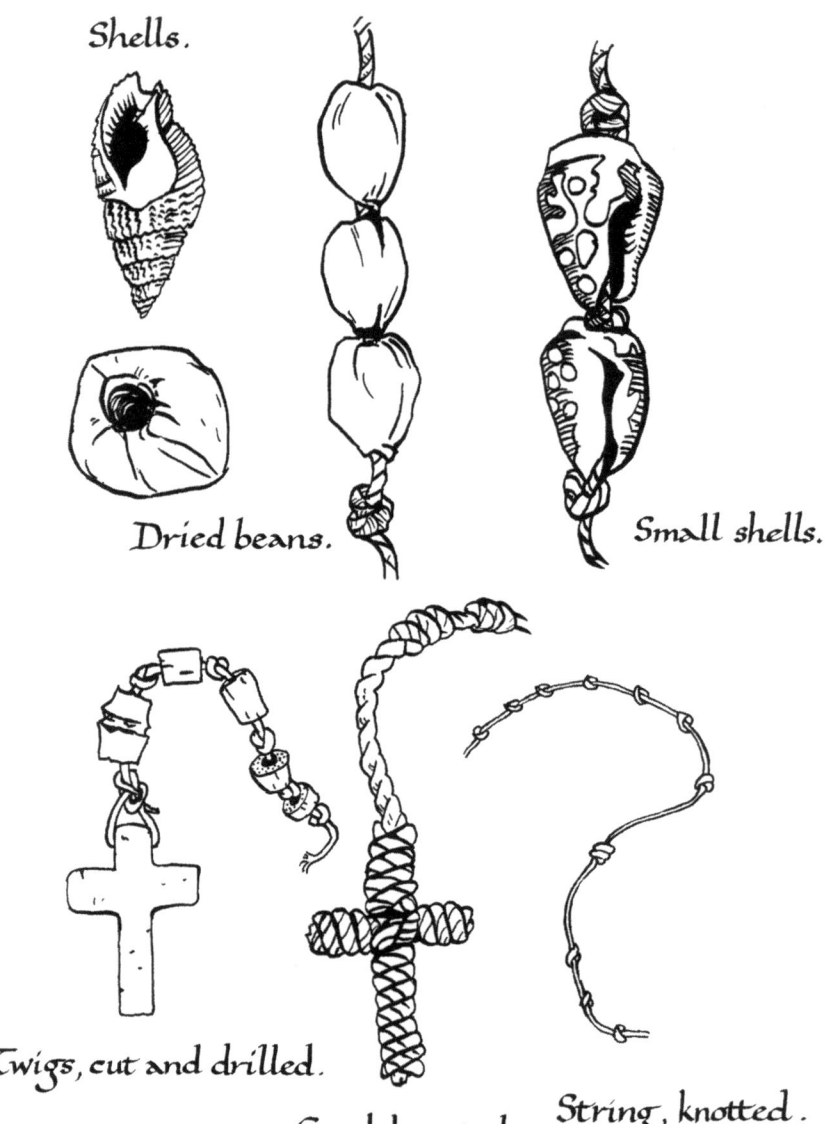

Dried beans.

Small shells.

Twigs, cut and drilled.

Cord, knotted.

String, knotted.

If you are to make a rosary, why not dedicate each bead as you thread it, with an individual prayer intention. In this way you will never forget to offer prayer for deceased friends and relatives and for your own family members, and you will not be distracted from your meditation on the mysteries. Even if you fail to remember whom the individual beads are dedicated for, God will not fail to recall your requests.

Securing a crucifix.

THE HISTORY OF THE ROSARY

The word 'rosary' would originally have meant a 'rose garden.' Only later did the name become applied to a book of devotions, such as Our Lady's Psalter. The word 'bead' originally meant 'a prayer.'

The use of garlands of beads to facilitate the rhythm and counting of prayer goes back into antiquity. There is, for instance, evidence of such strings of beads as far back as in the religion of ancient Nineveh. We know that prayer strings bearing thirty-three, sixty-six or ninety-nine beads, were seen by Marco Polo during his travels in the early 13th century. These particular prayer beads were used by the Moslems to devotedly count the ninety-nine names of Allah. The early Franciscans found that prayer beads were in common use among the Buddhists of Japan.

The early Christian hermits used pebbles, a cribbage-type board, or a heavy cord with knots or beads in order to count short prayers like the 'Jesus prayer.' The two ends of these cords were sometimes joined together. Outside of monastic life, however, the prayer cord was not much in evidence and it was Christians returning from the East who popularised the rosary in Western Europe.

In the eleventh century, monks and lay brothers who were unable to recite the 150 psalms through situation or illiteracy, were required to say a corresponding number of Our Fathers instead.

In the eleventh century, Lady Godiva of Coventry described her own treasured prayer beads as the 'circlet of precious stones which she had threaded on a cord, in order that, by fingering them one after another, she might count her prayers exactly.' On her death around 1075 she left this prayer cord to a statue of Our Lady.

But those prayers were not yet 'Hail Marys.' Throughout the Middle Ages, such strings of beads were known as 'Paternosters'. The rosary is still known as a Paternoster in some languages. Fifty 'Paters' became known as a 'rosary' and one hundred and fifty 'Paters' were known as a 'Psalter.'

The first part of the Hail Mary appears in the sixth century in the East and a century later in the West, but was only widely known in the later part of the eleventh century. Brought to our notice by St. Peter Damian, who died 1072, it was to have become popular a century later. It received further prominence in the year 1198, when it was decided that the faithful should be taught the 'Creed,' the 'Our Father' and the 'Ave.'

As the greetings of the Archangel Gabriel and of St. Elizabeth are salutations rather than prayers, they lend themselves well to repetition, and when the Ave became popular, the rosary was already on hand as a counter.

Because the Ave was a salutation, it was common, in East and West, to accompany each recitation with a bow or genuflection. The Ancren Riwle, which was published before 1200 AD, suggests fifty Aves, with prostrations, in sets of ten. The contemporary biographer of St. Albert the Great (1206-1280) tells us that 'A hundred times a day he bent his knees, while he repeated each time 'Hail Mary, full of grace, the Lord is with thee: Blessed art thou among women, and blessed is the fruit of thy womb.' The text is given in full, an indication that it was still not universally familiar. The addition to the salutation of the holy name of 'Jesus,' dates from the mid thirteenth century. And so the salutation ended.

Because the Ave, so far, was a salutation, it was only natural to add a prayer. St Bernadine of Siena is known to have once added the words 'Holy Mary, mother of God, pray for us'. But the last part in its full form appears first in a little book by Savonarola in 1495.

The shorter form of the Ave still survived in Ireland until the end of the last century, as there the latter part of the Ave was looked on as a separate prayer.

Two Carthusians were responsible for developing the rosary further. Around the year 1365, Henry of Kalkar, grouped the 150 Aves into decades preceded by an Our Father. Then in about 1409, Dominic of Prussia, proposed contemplating mysteries of the Faith while saying the prayers.

At the close of the fifteenth century, there were still no set subjects for meditation. The original proposal was to meditate on a different point while saying each Ave. Yet this was only possible for those who could read, and although printing had been invented, a book of one hundred and fifty illustrations was not practicable. So during the sixteenth century, the subjects were reduced to one for each decade and books of woodcut illustrations were produced for the benefit of those who could not read.

LOURDES

The subjects that we now use for meditation in the Holy Rosary, appear in 1483, in a book called 'Our Dear Lady's Psalter.' Published by a Dominican, there were still some differences. These were that the 14th decade was then the 'Assumption' and the 15th decade was the 'Last Judgement.' In the sixteenth century this arrangement prevailed, with the addition of the 'Glory be' at the end of each decade. The subjects now became known as 'Mysteries'.

But a rosary surviving with a slightly different configuration can be seen on the statue of the 'Crowned Virgin' in the 'Domaine' in Lourdes and also St.Bernadette's own rosary, housed in the museum close by. This is the 'Brigittine Rosary,' having six decades on a string instead of the normal five. Promoted by the Carmelite order, it follows a slightly different pattern of prayer, with an extra decade on each circuit.

Prayer beads are not only an ancient tradition but can be ecumenically used to great effect. Plain rosaries, made of wood and without a cross, were used by Charles de Foucauld in the early 1900s amongst those he met of Muslim Faith. 'My God, I love you' was said on the small beads, and 'My God, I love you with all my heart' on the large ones. Surely there cannot be a more beautiful, simple and pleasing prayer.

When, in 1917 Our Lady appeared to the three shepherd children at Fatima, she asked the children to 'pray the Rosary every day in honour of Our Lady of the Rosary, in order to obtain peace for the world and an end to the war, because only she can help you.'

And she requested: 'When you pray the Rosary, say after each mystery:

'O my Jesus, forgive us our sins, save us from the fire of hell. Lead all souls to heaven, especially those who are in most need of thy mercy.' These words have become known the 'Fatima Prayer.'

Many great saints have influenced the use and popularity of the Holy Rosary, of whom St.Dominic and St.Louis de Montfort are notable examples.

In the year 2002 Pope John Paul II added the 'Mysteries of Light' to the rosary meditations, and the rosary appeared complete, with a new set of subjects for meditation, covering the public life and miracles of Jesus. The Pope called us earnestly to rediscover the treasures hidden in the rosary and to pray the rosary daily, for our families and for world peace.

The beauty of the rosary is that it can be used as a medium through which meditations can be added or combined as personal prayer demands. The occasional substitution of a new theme into the decades, maybe for instance adding the 'Visit of the Magi' in place of the 'Presentation' or of combining the 'Assumption' and the 'Coronation of Our Lady' as has been done in the past, leaves room for a decade of personal choice.

Since 1920, variations have been put forward in order to revive the ancient practice of devoting a different thought, not just to each decade, but to each individual 'Ave.' The most well loved of these being the 'Scriptural Rosary'. The 'Crown of Thorns Rosary' is a new example of this variation.

ABOUT THE ARTISTS

Philip Hagreen

Philip Hagreen was born in Berkshire in 1890. As he grew up, he spent much time amongst the fishing communities of the Suffolk coast, where he eagerly learnt the skills of the country folk around him. He loved God and he loved His creation. Philip became a well known wood engraver and watercolour artist. However, when his sight began to fail as the result of cataract, his means of earning a living to support his wife and young family was threatened. Under the guidance of his wife Aileen, the family travelled to Lourdes on pilgrimage to ask Our Lady for a cure. Their ardent prayer was granted.

Although invalided out of two world wars, Philip still humorously recalled having to wear a pair of spurs whilst riding an early army motorbike. He lived till he was 98, still avidly corresponding with the Times and the Tablet. Although bed bound for the last ten years of his life, he never grumbled. His mind remained sharp and his voice stayed as clear as his bright blue eyes. Stories of his adventures at the helm of a three masted topsail schooner whilst fetching ice from glaciers with which to pack fish, and of a flight in an early biplane, were as memorable as his singing of an ancient sea-shanty.

Philip loved people, never judged them and found amusement in all, even in the most difficult of personalities, giving each the credence of being of God's special creation. He lived for peace.

John Paul de Quay

John Paul is the great grandson of Philip Hagreen.

John Paul has updated his great grandfather's woodcut illustrations for the Holy Rosary by producing new 'pen and ink' drawings for the newly added 'Mysteries of Light.' Other illustrations by John Paul include those for 'Praying the Rosary' and for 'Thoughts on making a Rosary'. The rosaries depicted on these pages were handmade by Philip Hagreen.

John Paul has illustrated other work for Crown of Thorns and his greatest interest lies in animation.

About the Authors / Compilers

Lisa de Quay

Co-founder of the charity 'Crown of Thorns' Lisa has worked with dioceses worldwide in the promotion of the Holy Rosary and in humanitarian aid. She is married and has five children, four adult sons and a daughter.

Lisa is the granddaughter of the artist Philip Hagreen and has inherited his love of the countryside, her knowledge of shepherding being inspirational in the formation of this book.

Dudley Plunkett

Dudley Plunkett is Senior Tutor at the Maryvale Institute. He is married, with two children and three grandchildren. He has written extensively about Marian topics and also about evangelisation, for example *Heaven wants to be Heard* (Gracewing, 1997) and *Saving Secular Society* (Alive Publishing, 2007).

Fr. John Hagreen

Son of Philip and Aileen Hagreen, John lived in Lourdes for six years of his childhood and gained a great understanding of Marian devotion. On returning to England he attended Ampleforth School and when called up into military duty, he served as a captain in the infantry.

On active duty one night, John felt a lady's hand on his shoulder, pulling him gently backwards. As soon as he had stepped back, a shell exploded exactly where he had been standing. His life having been spared, John studied for the priesthood at Wonersh Seminary and was ordained in 1952.

LIST OF PLATES

All illustrations are by Philip Hagreen unless otherwise stated as the work of John Paul de Quay. Portraits are by the family of the artists.   All artwork remains strictly copyright©.

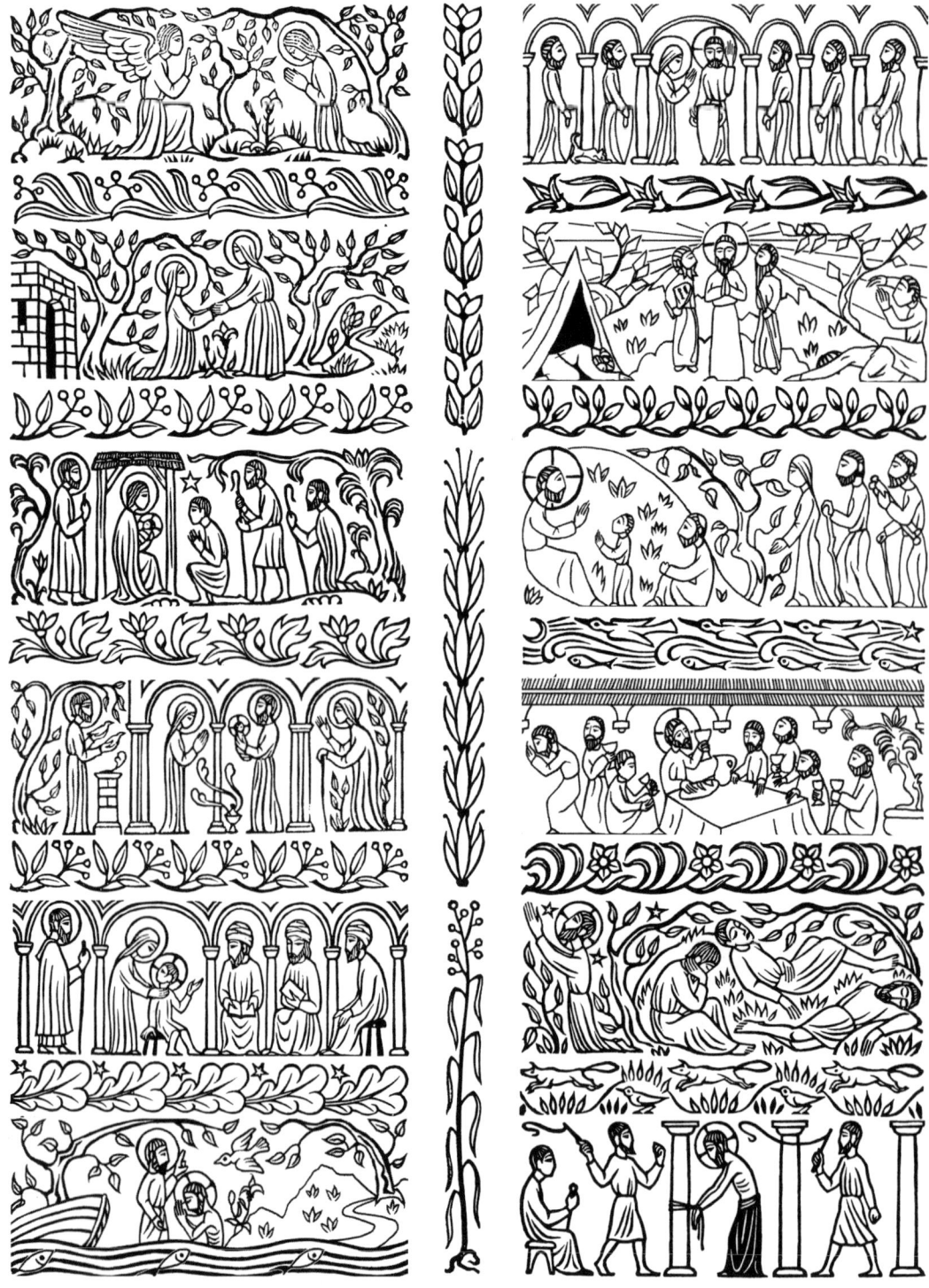